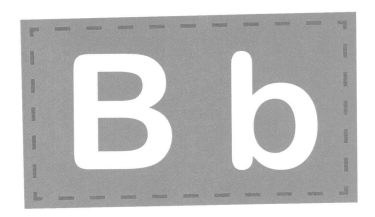 is for...

EL BALÓN

Let's Learn

By Sachin Sachdeva

 is for...

AMBULANCIA

 is for...

LA CEREZA

 is for...

EL DULCES

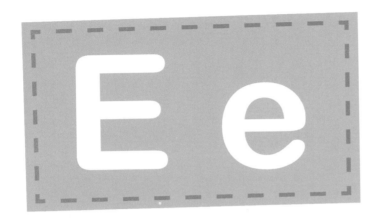 is for...

EL EXCAVADORA

 is for...

LA FLOR

 is for...

GRUA

 is for...

 is for...

LA IGUANA

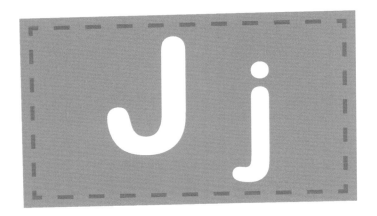 is for...

EL JEEP

 is for...

KAYAC

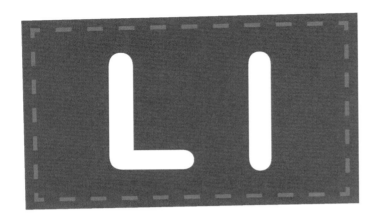 is for...

LA LÁMPARA

 is for...

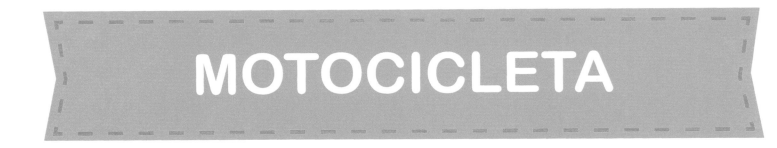
MOTOCICLETA

 is for...

LA NARANJA

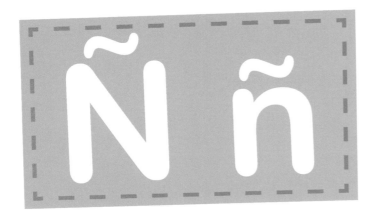 is for...

LA BAÑERA

O o is for...

LA OVEJA

 is for...

EL PESCADO

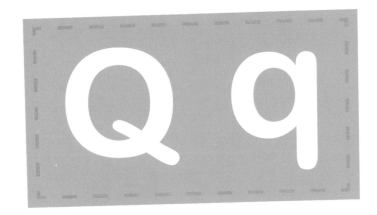 is for...

EL QUESO

 is for...

RODILLO DE CAMINOS

 is for...

SUBMARINO

 is for...

LA TELE

 is for...

UNICICLO

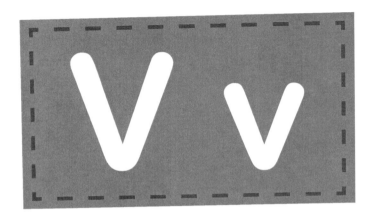 is for...

LA VACA

 is for...

EL WAFLE

 is for...

XEBEC

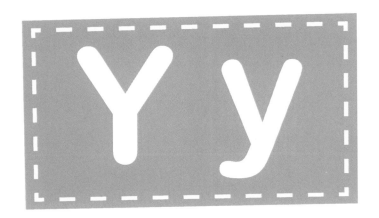 is for...

EL YATE

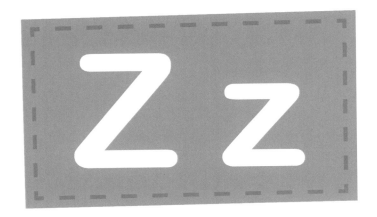 is for...

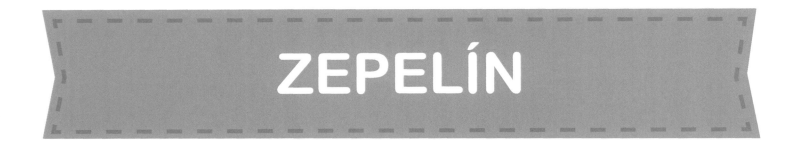

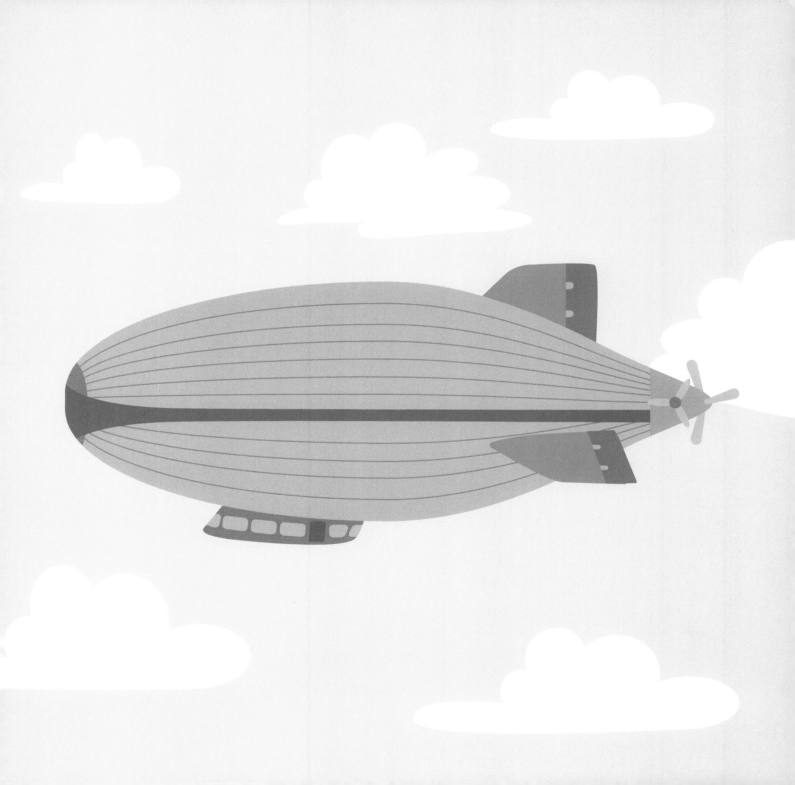

Now let's do it again!

A B C D E

F G H I J K

L M N Ñ Ñ O

P Q R S T U

V W X Y Z

If your child love this book, i have one more **ABC book of Animals** in Spanish. It has beautiful illustrations of animals which kids will love to explore and learn at the same time.

Thank you - Sachin Sachdeva (Author & Illustrator)

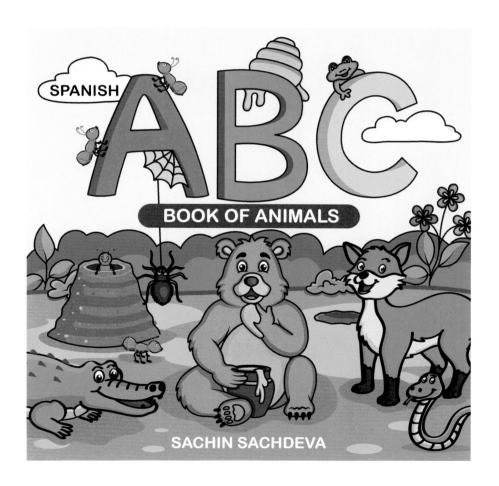

Available on all Amazon stores

Ta-Da, Bye Bye, Love you...
Keep Smiling...

Made in the USA
Middletown, DE
15 March 2019